Best Wishes

Jim Palmer

THE BEGINNING OF THE LAW

by JIM POULTER

Illustrated by
Andrea Cameron
and
Denise Corboy

The story of original journey
to the land where the Spirit of Life was resting

First published 1992
RED HEN ENTERPRISES
278 Serpells Rd
Templestowe 3106
Victoria Australia
ph (03) 842 3598

National Library of Australia
Cataloguing-in-Publication Data

Poulter, Jim
The Beginning of The Law
ISBN 0 949196 03 7
1. Aborigines Australian — Migrations — Folklore
2. Aborigines, Australian — Religion — Juvenile literature
I — Cameron, Andrea 1969– II Corboy, Denise 1967– III Title
398.2049915

Produced by Island Graphics
Typeset by Bookset
Printed in Singapore

IN CELEBRATION
OF THE HERITAGE WE ALL SHARE
AS AUSTRALIANS

— the oldest continent
and the birthplace of human society

Bunjil sat at his usual spot near the cave entrance. His arms were folded across his knees and his sharpened spear lay across his lap. Bunjil's dark eyes glinted from the shadow of his heavy brow, as he looked out from the cave. He watched a distant eagle silhouetted against the red evening sky. It was the bird that he had been named after.

Bunjil looked back into the cave where the light of the cooking fire threw people's flickering shadows on the far wall. It was a good cave. No smoke in the eyes. He briefly watched the smoke curling up to the vent hole in the ceiling, as his mate Tuppoon prodded the carcass of the roasting animal. It smelt good.

Bunjil stared at his heavily pregnant wife. Tuppoon was a good mate. A good mother to their two sons. And smart too. He took Tuppoon as his mate, because he knew she was smart like him. Her eyes told him she was smart.

When he looked at her eyes, he always thought of the water lilies she was named after. Maybe their third child would be a girl with eyes like her mother.

Bunjil's heavy brow creased in a frown as he looked out again toward the gathering gloom. The night animals were starting to roam. Bunjil rose and cautiously looked out, spear at the ready. His friend Tuan moved up next to him, club in hand, and also looked out.

Nothing. But good to make sure.

The air outside was already cold. When he was young the nights were not so cold. Old ones said that once there were no white mountains.

Tuan nudged Bunjil and pointed to a big prowling cat down the slope. Bunjil moved out from the cave mouth and picked up a rock. He hurled it, striking the big cat heavily on the ear. With a snarl of pain it loped away. Tuan laughed and slapped his friend on the shoulder. No-one could throw rocks like Bunjil.

The two men moved back into the cave entrance and sat down once more. Tuan's oldest boy Woonit asked what was there. His father laughed, saying it was just a cat with a sore head.

Bunjil smiled at Tuan's joke. He was good to be with. Tuan was the only one who had stood behind him when he fought Mundarra to be leader of the tribe. And Tuan was the one who told him how to win. Throw rocks.

Bunjil was strong, but Mundarra was much bigger, much stronger. So Bunjil made sure they fought where rocks were plenty. He ran around and threw rocks until Mundarra was hurt. Then he bashed his brain out.

Remembering the fight made Bunjil breathe deeply. He looked at his hand and moved his fingers as if to grasp a rock. He threw rocks good because of his hand. He could move his thumb better than anyone. It helped him do things better.

Things like not letting go when someone tried to take something away from you. Like grasping a club strong. Nobody could knock a club from his grasp, but he could do it to them. He could do little things better too, like picking up seeds.

Only Tuan's son and his own children had a hand like him.

The grip had helped him become the best hunter in the tribe. It looked like Tuan's son would be a good hunter too. Maybe if Tuppoon and he had a daughter next, young Woonit would be a good mate for her.

He already knew what his daughter's name would be. Wagara, after the smartest bird, the Crow. Because she would be smart, just like her mother.

Tuan rubbed his hands together as at last their two women began to dismember the roasted animal. Bunjil signalled for them to feed the children first. He smiled as the youngsters pushed close to the fire, gasping as they handled the hot scraps of flesh.

Tuppoon then tore a leg from the carcass and brought it to Bunjil. He stroked her wrist in thanks as she handed it to him.

She smiled and he thought of the water lilies.

Wagara stood on the clifftop, the wind ruffling the fur of her cloak. Her coal black eyes were fixed on the eagle high above the sea.

It was Bunjil, the powerful bird that bore her father's name.

Surely it must be a sign.

At the edge of the horizon she could see land. Bunjil rose ever higher in the sky and moved out toward the distant land. Soon it was no more than a speck.

Yes, it was a sign.

Wagara motioned to her twin sons who waited behind. They were the best hunters in the tribe, like their grandfather had been. She had led the tribe since Bunjil's death so long ago, and it was through her sons that Wagara's word was enforced.

Kappetch and Koorokitch came and stood next to their mother. She pointed to the land on the horizon.

That was their journey's end.

The two young men clapped each other on the shoulder in excitement. They had never made such a journey before across open water. But the prospect held no fears. During their years of journey along the coast, they had often made fishing rafts of bamboo.

Wagara watched as her sons made their way down the sandy cliff trail to the rest of the tribe.

Everything they did was always as one. They were like two halves. This was why Wagara had named them after the Black Cockatoo and the White Cockatoo.

Wagara once again looked to the distant land. She sighed. So many years of journey. Her mother Tuppoon had told her many times, how the journey had begun as soon as she was born more than forty summers ago.

Bunjil had seen that the cold was creeping closer. He knew that the tribe would have to move south toward the sun.

He had decided this when he saw an owl fly in the daytime.

So the journey began after Wagara was born. Always travelling with the midday sun on their faces. Sometimes they stayed at good places for a few months, especially when babies were to be born. But then they moved on again.

Wagara could no longer see the eagle over the sea. Bunjil was waiting for them in the new land under the sun. He would protect them. Just like he had protected them when they crossed the white mountains.

Kappetch and Koorokitch had only been young boys then, but they still talked about how their grandfather had fought the big snow cat and saved them.

And how the fire from the sky had split the tree where he died.

Without the snow cat to eat and the fire from the tree to warm them, they would all have died on the white mountain.

Now, just four families waited for their final journey. Two rafts would be enough to carry them. Koorokitch would care for one half of the tribe and Kapetch would care for the other half.

That had been her first rule.

Each of her sons to be responsible for a half of the tribe. Then after that she had made the rules on who would be mates.

Only Wagara made the rules. Kappetch and Koorokitch made sure they were followed. They knew her rules were good, like their grandfather's rules.

But Wagara also knew from Bunjil that she had to be both smart and strong. When her older brother had challenged her rules and tried to be leader, she knew his rules would not be good.

So she had ordered his death and her young sons had carried out the order without question.

But who would make the rules when she died?

Wagara nodded to herself as she stared from the clifftop. When they reached the new land she must talk with all the tribe. They must all decide together.

Rules must be good enough to live past their makers.

Once there was nothing
Nothing but the Spirit of All Life

For a long time there was nothing
Then in the mind of the Spirit of Life
A Dreaming began

And in this Dreaming the world took shape

Fire Wind and Rain
Earth and Sky Land and Sea

The Great Being Dreamed of all these things

And the Creation Dreaming took so long
That the Spirit of Life began to grow tired

But the Great Spirit liked the Dream
And wanted the Dream to continue

So Spirit Creatures were sent into the Dream
And the Secret of Dreaming was sent with them

But before entering the land to rest
The spirits of all children yet to be born
Were created by the great Spirit

So that the Secret of Dreaming could be passed on

And this is why the spirits of all children
Must wait in the Dreamtime
To be found in a Dream by their fathers

A Dream that will guide the Spirit Child
To the body of their mother

Who will make their flesh

Being now very tired from the long Dreaming
The Spirit of Life entered the Land to rest

At a warm and green place called Meralmedah

And so it was in this place of First Dreaming
That all the Creator Spirits gathered

But so too did the evil spirit Morpor

Morpor was from the darkness before the Dreaming
And wanted the Dreaming to Die

So Morpor took the form of the Owl
Spread his wings
And rose up toward the sun

Soon his shadow stretched across all Meralmedah
And the Spirit of Life could not rest

So the Spirit of Life withdrew from the Land
And a great cold spread over it

Seeing Morpor turn his eyes from the fire
Wagara the Crow kept the firestick safe

She told Kappatch the Black Cockatoo
And Koorokitch the White Cockatoo
To lead the journey out from Morpor's shadow

So Kappetch and Koorokitch led the way
And found where the Spirit of Life now rested

They led the other Creator spirits into the new land
Forming the landscape with their bodies
As they went along their Dreamtime Pathways

And when they had finished their work
They gave their Spirits up and took the forms
Of the animals and landmarks we see today

But Wagara knew there was one final task

She knew that to take care of the Land
And for the Spirit of Life to rest safely

Proper ritual must be made
To pass on the Dreaming Secrets

So Wagara Dreamed and in this Dreaming
The world was of two halves

And she saw that in these halves
Was the balance of all things

Day and Night   Heat and Cold
Man and Woman   Spirit and Flesh

Each was a half of the same whole

So Wagara the Crow told of her Dreaming
And instructed Kappetch and Koorokitch

That they were to each guard one half of the Dreaming

And from Wagara's Dreaming it was also told
That care of the Spirit and of the Flesh

Were to be separate duties between man and woman

And so it became the duty of men
To have first care of the Spirit
And to pass this duty on to their sons

So also it became the duty of women
To have first care of the Flesh

And to pass this duty on to their daughters

This then was the Beginning of the Law

ABOUT THIS STORY

Commonly, Aboriginal Dreamtime stories are recounted without any attempt at explanation of the totemic symbols used. Sometimes there is an attempt to convey underlying morals, but most often the stories are presented as simple but colourful animal stories.

They are of course much more than that. They are also more than just cautionary tales or stories of morals and manners. As is tried to convey with the dual versions of The Beginning of the Law, they are often also codified tribal histories. Dreamtime stories are often records of real events and real issues, as they affected real people.

In writing The Beginning of the Law, I have therefore drawn on themes from many Dreamtime stories from different parts of Australia. The reader will see from the story, that concepts of the Garden of Eden or of Paradise Lost, are not unique to Judeo–Christian faiths. Many Australian Aboriginal stories tell of mythical places such as Meralmedah, where ancestoral beings first gathered.

Stories of subsequent journey and creation by these heroic figures are also repetitive themes within Dreamtime legends. These stories of the work of Creator Spirits, can however be seen as stories of original migration.

The mentalistic nature of Aboriginal religion, indicates that just as original creation occurred in the mind of the Spirit of Life, so creation was only complete when it was finally witnessed by the human mind. The Beginning of the Law therefore draws on these themes to recount the beginnings of human society in Australia.

The dramatic version however is also informed by recent genetic and archeological research. This clearly establishes Australian Aborigines as the oldest race in the world and the stock from which every other race is therefore descended. Homo Sapiens ultimately arose through a fortunate linkage of higher intelligence with the fully opposable thumb, and the story tells how this unrepresentative group from a pre-human society, finally found their way into Australia.

As marsupial animals cannot communicate disease to humans, these original settlers fortuitously found themselves in a virtually disease free environment, and without serious predatory competitors. Population was thus able to flourish, and the first human culture developed. The timing of this first arrival, I place as during an Ice Age around 160,000 years ago.

By using a European dramatic style in the initial story, then using a totemic style in the subsequent version, it is intended to convey something of the deeper symbolism inherent in all Dreamtime stories, as well as my own beliefs on how the first human society began in Australia.

It is important to know for instance, that in many tribes the Eagle is a totem for strength or power. In some tribes it is also a symbol of human brotherhood. In the earliest times however, it seems reasonable to assume that people took their names from the creatures around them. From there, the personality and achievements of the person became intertwined and ultimately indivisible from that of the animal itself.

In the story, Bunjil is a tribal leader who leads his people on their migratory journey away from an impending ice age. During the long journey, Bunjil sacrifices his life to save the others. Bunjil thus symbolises the power, nobility and brotherhood of the Eagle.

A second fairly universal totem used in the story, is that of the Owl, which is often used to represent death. The casting of Morpor's shadow over Meralmedah, forbodes the coming death of the land. Later, the spectre of death is kept at bay when Wagara utilises fire. This of course marks a highly significant point in human history, when fire becomes a conscious tool and a powerful weapon for survival. The discovery and use of fire is also of course a pervasive theme of many Dreamtime legends.

A third common totem is that of the Crow, which in many tribes represents wisdom. Wagara shows her wisdom, by perceiving that the world is divided into complementary opposites. This concept is a cornerstone of Aboriginal philosophy, and is similar to but predates, the ancient Chinese concepts of Yin and Yang.

These halves into which the world is divided are called moieties. these moieties are symbolised in most Aboriginal tribes by the totems of Black Cockatoo and White Cockatoo, but sometimes by Crow and Eagle. The relationship of Crow and Eagle also symbolises the necessity for power and wisdom to be kept in balance.

In the end, the story conveys that the First Law sought to embody the idea of universal duality. This was seen as a means of ensuring that balance was maintained in the harvesting of the earth's resources. In the story, this was done by dividing all hunting and protective responsibilities between Kappatch and Koorokitch.

As also indicated in the story, other rules then flowed from this basic division into moieties. This included dividing the primary spiritual and secular responsibilities between men and women.

This separation between spiritual and secular is another crucial concept that underlies Aboriginal social organisation. It is symbolised by male responsibility for 'finding' a child's spirit before it is born, and the woman's responsibility for making the child's flesh. That is, men have primary spiritual responsibility and women a primary responsibility for day to day matters of care.

In actual fact the division into spiritual and secular responsibilities is not as simple as that, as men and women have both spiritual and secular responsibilities. However it is an important principal that allows the authority of men and women to be carefully balanced out. For instance, allocation of mothers-in-law and consequently of wives, were always within the authority of the women. It is therefore a fallacy to believe that Aboriginal society is male dominated.

This then according to the story, is the basis of the Law. From the division of all things into opposites, a complex set of laws developed gradually, to govern every facet of life and relationship. These laws and relationships have been symbolised by specific animals, and coded into legend and story so that it provided an instructive basis for daily life.

The totemic examples used in this story, represent only a tiny fraction of the whole system, but my own understanding does not extend far past that expressed in the story. Hopefully though, this will provide some food for thought to the reader in trying to interpret the deeper meanings of other Dreamtime stories.

Jim Poulter